IATEM IIIIIII
I0123755

Ship Repair Project Manager's Guide

Eng. Mohammed Khamis Mohammed

Professional Ship Repair Project Manager & Independent Marine Surveyor Consultancy.

FOREWORD

A Ship Repair - Project Manager without guidance and project management tools is like a ship without rudder and propeller

-Fernando Remolina, PMP

A ship without rudder and propeller can't arrive at a safe port and probably will get lost at sea. Also, depending on multiple conditions, it can sink. If you are working as a Ship Repair Manager, you probably don't want your project to get lost or just sink. Eng. Mohammed Khamis, in his book, will give a step-by-step guide for ship repair managers to avoid mishaps happening to their ship repair projects.

This book is especially for:
• Students interested in starting a career in Ship Repair.
• Beginner Ship Repair Managers who wish to better understand the process.
• Seasoned Ship Repair Managers - as a reminder of forgotten aspects of the daily tasks.

Eng. Mohammed Khamis, in his book, uses all of his vast experience (in ship repair, ship conversion, and drydocking recognized by different ship owners and shipyards around the world) to explain the functions of a Ship Repair Manager on a daily basis along with his relationship with shipyard organization, the ship's owner representative and the service engineer who attends a ship repair project. He summarizes his experience of fifteen years in the following chapters:

Chapter 1: Ship Repair Yards General Terms Definitions
Chapter 2: Familiarization with Ship Repair Yard Main Departments
Chapter 3: Familiarization with Standard Ship Repair Specifications
Chapter 4: Familiarization with the Project Management Procedures
Chapter 5: Familiarization with The Form in use Related Projects
Chapter 6: How to build your experience as a ship repair manager?
Chapter 7: Ship Crew Duties Prior to Entering the Drydock.
Chapter 8: Ship Crew Duties During the Repair & Dry Dock

I highly recommend this book, which will help people interested and/or working as a Ship Repair Manager to understand how to act and react while working in a shipyard. The information given in this book is not taught in a university but only learned through experience and Mohamed Khamis is sharing his valuable experience with all readers.

Fernando Remolina, PMP
Senior Project Manager
Book Author: Shipyard Project Management

Introduction

Ship repair activities are considered the heart and focus of interest at any ship yard. The main purpose of this guide is to make available to all ship repair yard managements and their ship repair managers (SRM) a ready reference. The role of ship repair yard management should be considered by ship repair managers as very important in staying aware that he is the yard's representative to the ship owner in the project he is handling.

To assist all new ship repair managers in performing their daily activities, I have written this guide book based on my own practical work experiences. It is my hope that ship repair managers everywhere will benefit from this guide.

Eng. Mohammed Khamis Mohammed
Bachelor's Degree of Marine and Naval Architecture Engineering
Alexandria University,
Faculty of Engineering,
Egypt.

Experienced: Professional Ship Repair Project Manager | Independent Marine Surveyor Consultancy.

About the Author

Professional Projects Manager and Independent Marine Surveyor Consultancy of Ship Building | Ship Repair | Dry Docking | Ship Conversions | Ports and Shipping | Offshore Oil Rigs | Oil and Gas | Maritime Industry.

Eng. Mohamed Khamis
engkhames@yahoo.com

Bachelor's Degree of Marine and Naval Architecture Engineering
Egyptian | Birth Date: 20.02.1976 | Living in Oman.

has vast, rich experiences worldwide in marketing of ship building, ship repair, dry docking, offshore, ship conversions, oil rigs and maritime industry with strong familiarization in the project management, yard production and operation management, tendering and estimation, technical resource optimization, manpower mobilization, cost control, international maritime organization requirements and rules application with focusing on QA/QC and HSE rules and regulations.
He has worked in different international reputable companies such as:

6

(ASRY) Arab Shipbuilding and Repair Yard | Bahrain
(ODC) Oman Drydock Company | Oman
(ASY) Alexandria Ship Yard | Egypt
(ENC) Egyptian Navigation Company | Egypt
(ESRBC) Egyptian Ship Repair and Building | Egypt
(EAMS) Egyptian Authority for Maritime Safety | Egypt
Mahoney Shipping Company | Egypt
Al Shanfari Marine Services LLC | Oman

Table of Contents

9

Register This Book

Thank you very much for purchasing this book. First of all, before you read ahead, please **register your book** here and get for FREE the Excel templates/forms included in this book: https://projectmanagers.org/ship-repair-book-registration

As a **ProjectManagers.Org Ship Repair Book Club** member, you will receive lots of benefits and support from our Book Club Forum:
https://projectmanagers.org/ship-repair-book-club

Certification Program

This is the official book for taking the **ProjectManagers.Org Certified Ship Repair Project Manager (SRPM)** program:

https://projectmanagers.org/ship-repair-certification
This Career Program will improve your job opportunities and certify your skills gained from this book.

The Certification Exam is online, and once you sign up you can take it whenever you want (no deadline limits). Just sign up today for your exam and start enjoying this book.

Chapter 1: Ship Repair Yard General Terms and Definitions

1.1. Ship Yard

The organization for or in relation to ship repair, conversion, maintenance & reconstruction using yard facilities, personnel and equipment as an entity performing the work inside the dry dock, on berth, at anchorage area.

1.2. Customer/Owner

Any person, ship owner, ship management or ship operator who has agreed to the work with the yard in accordance with a contract.

1.3. Customer/Owner Representative

a party or parties duly authorized by the customer to act on behalf of the customer, with whom the yard may consult at all reasonable times and whose instructions, requests, and decisions are issued.

1.4. Vessel

Any ship, barge, rig or other marine craft which is to be subject of work.

1.5. Customer Staff/Ship Crew

The party or parties responsible for the operation of customer equipment.

1.6. Customer/Ship Repair Specification

A technical description of the work used as a basis for preparation of tender.

1.7. Tender

A quotation covering price, time, and terms to carry out work as described in the customer's specification.

1.8. Work

All tasks to be performed by the yard in accordance with customer specifications, including all changes of scope as agreed with a customer representative.

1.9. Project

Any contracted work between the yard and customer for performance of ship repair, conversion, docking, and related services.

1.10. Work Specification

A technical description of work as described in the customer's specification with reservation, exclusions, conditions, and remarks introduced by the tender and agreed according to the contract.

1.11. Yard Representative/Ship Repair Manager

the party or parties nominated by the yard to liaise between customer representative and yard for leading, coordinating, and managing the performance of specific projects is generally identified as the ship repair manager.

1.12. Yard Safety Rules

A set of safety rules and procedures based on international standards, local government rules, and common practices, binding to the customer and compulsory to the yard.

1.13. Class

The classification society bureau, whose rules and regulations will be applicable to a contract.

Chapter 2: Familiarization with Ship Repair Yard Main Departments

At any ship yard when it recruits a new Ship Repair Manager, yard policies are required to give him a familiarization period between three or four weeks. This is done to allow all new SRMs to become familiar with yard facilities, abilities, capabilities, persons in-charge, departments manuals, departments activities, and yard policies.

I consider this section of the book as your familiarization stage in the yard; therefore, let's go visit the main departments of the ship repair yard.

2.1. Human Resource Department

The HR Department is a critical component of employee in any business, no matter how small and this section has been produced in order to introduce to SRM the HR sections responsibilities include payroll, benefits, hiring, training, compensating and keeping up to date with the labor laws.

Main Role & Responsibility

The HR Department aligns the company's overall workforce strength to yearly plans and talent management. It introduces effective training plans (IDP), workforce management, employee and company compliance/laws and regulations. Lastly, it maintains

19

employment data and records, benefits administration, and workers' compensation.

Planning & Recruitment Section

- To formulate, recommend, and interpret rules, policies, and procedures such as the HR employee manual.

- Identify legal requirements and government regulations affecting human resource functions and advise the HR administration for effective implementation.

- Remain responsible for manpower demand analysis and on time supply of manpower.

- To make service level agreements with each department and update policies and procedures.

- To get the best employees by recruiting through appropriate modes in conjunction with service level agreements.

- To offer the best package/compensation of competitive wages and benefits to employees in line with company grading structure.

- To set appraisal policy to be linked with individual employee targets which contribute overall to the Department's KPI's.

- To advise and facilitate for effective employee engagement to each department, effectively keeping attrition rate at minimum level.

- To keep departmental cost at a minimum level (overall cost including manpower).

Personal Section
- To release salaries and other benefits to employees on time.

- To maintain the human resources database of employees, salaries, wage adjustments, and wage rates.

- To set up the administration of the company's benefits and award program.

- To control Insurance - employee related (i.e. medical, life, workmen compensation, etc. [policy, tender document, claim and reimbursement management]).

- To provide assistance to employees, supervisors, and managers about employee performance, discipline, supervision, and grievances in line with labor law and yard policies.

- To investigate complaints and recommendations of employees and then take appropriate action.

Training & Development Section
- Maintain responsibility for training development, career development, and sustaining high-performing employees.

- To manage and optimize the training budget.

- To prepare skill gap analysis and a training plan to minimize the gap in conjunction with a Performance Appraisal Report.

2.2. General Administration Department

The GA Department is important component to ensure the efficient performance of all departments' employees in the company and this section has been produced in order to introduce to SRM the GA sections responsibilities include the housing, transporting & entertainment.

Main Roles & Responsibilities
The GA Department provides services and the required necessities to external and internal customers; it supports all departments in the company and establishes policies and procedures based on company rules for proper and organized flow for raising efficiency.

Administration & Planning Section

- To plan, organize service for ship owners and other departments.

- To establish and maintain administrative policies and procedures, asset controls, archive and document control.

- To complete tenancy renewal formalities with sub-contractors.

- Manage and organize property documents including the tenancy agreement and assets list.

- To prepare the annual budget of GA and set budget controls to achieve cost saving targets.

- Supervise writing, editing, and arrangement for production of newsletters, in-house magazines, reports, brochures, advertisements, translations of letters, publication of diaries, and calendars.

- Disseminate received information to concerned yard departments.

- Physically verify at the end of each quarter and liaise with internal and external auditors for asset verifications.

Housing, Catering & Transportation Section

- Plan, organize, and coordinate the functions of transportation.

- To hire and supervise cars and buses; to set and monitor transpiration policies.

- Coordinate routine maintenance and maintain related records.

- Monitor vehicle registrations, renewal, and traffic violations along with vehicle accident claims.

- To complete the tenancy agreement with sub-contractors and maintain or keep records for other incomes.

- Plan, organize, and maintain hygiene dormitory, canteen, and health club.

- Maintain comprehensive records covering all aspects of the company's residential properties.

- To manage and maintain office facilities, furniture, and office environment; to keep the properties in excellent condition.

- Plan, organize, and provide best services of catering to employees, ship-owners, and guests.

Hospitality & Entertainment Section
- Ship-owner/Guest and VIP Protocol.
- Promote and publicize company events, celebrations, parties, and ceremonies.
- To provide support (entertainment facility, transportation, and accommodation) to ship owners in a related department.

2.3. Internal Audit Department

The Internal audit helps the company employees accomplish its objectives by bringing a systematic, disciplined approach to evaluate and improve the effectiveness of risk management, control and governance processes.

This section has been produced in order to introduce the IA responsibilities for SRM.

Main Roles & Responsibilities
The scope of internal audit encompasses, but is not limited to, the examination and evaluation of the adequacy and effectiveness of the organization's governance, risk management, and internal processes as well as the quality of performance in carrying out assigned responsibilities to achieve the organization's stated goals and objectives.

- Reviewing the reliability and integrity of financial and operational information and the means to identify, measure, classify and report such information.

- Reviewing the system established to ensure compliance with those policies, procedures, laws and regulations which could have a significant impact on the organization.

- Reviewing the means of safeguarding assets and as appropriate verifying the existence of such assets.

- Reviewing the effectiveness, efficiency, and economy with which resources are employed.

- Reviewing operations or programs to ascertain whether results are consistent with established objectives and goals and whether operations or programs are being carried out as planned.

- Performing consulting and advisory services related to governance, risk management, and control as appropriate for the organization.

- Reporting periodically to AC on the internal audit activity's purpose, authority, responsibility and performance relative to its plan.

- Reporting significant risk exposures and control issues, including fraud risk, governance issues, and other matters needed or requested by the AC and BOD.

- Evaluating specific operations at the request of the AC, BOD, or Top management as appropriate and reporting the result.

- Providing information periodically to AC on the status and results of the annual audit plan and the sufficiency of the department resources.

- Review application and general controls of IT system to ensure the reliability and integrity of information.

- Provide reasonable assurance regarding the reliability of financial report and the preparation of financial statements in accordance with internationally accepted accounting principles.

- Reviewing compliance to laws and regulations including Corporate Governance and CMA rules.

2.4. Corporate Strategy & Planning Department

A corporate strategy department functions as a coordinating body, developing and implementing strategies that satisfy the objectives of individual departments as well as promoting overall corporate goals.

This section has been produced in order to introduce the CS&P responsibilities for SRM.

Main Roles & Responsibilities

The CS&P Department sets up mid and long-term business plans with expansion and diversification plans, and it leads implementations of strategic priorities. It aligns the company's performance with vision and mission, explores the market to introduce new business opportunities, ensures shareholder's strategy/directions are adopted/incorporated in BP, managing governance issues, and policies.

- To map out and implement a strategy to achieve vision and goals.

- To formulate long/mid-term business plan based on a strategy.

- External/Internal Environment Scanning, SWOT Analysis, and Financial Forecast.

- To develop new opportunities to expand business areas.

- To conduct feasibility studies and execute business expansion and diversification.

- To prepare agenda to be discussed and shared in the weekly meeting of top management.

- To follow up on decisions made in the meeting and implement them in practice.

- To prepare reports for management's decision making as required.

- To set-up policies and keep the archive updated, aligning operational manuals.

- To maintain and supervise the "Manual of Authority"/governance policies.

- To set-up the plan and supervision of subsidiary companies, if any.

2.5. HSSE Department

SRM is responsible to ensure that safety precautions, security level, health & environment conditions during the ship stay in the ship yard for repair.
Safety induction to be given for new employed SRM and this section has been produced in order to introduce the HSSE responsibilities for SRM.

Main Roles & Responsibilities

The HSSE Department seeks to provide necessary HSSE information, HSSE planning and strategy for HSSE efficiency; it minimizes incidents and accidents by strengthening HSSE policy and control and establishes proper process and procedure for enhancing efficiency.

Health & Safety Section
- To develop and implement health and safety procedures.
- Safety control on-board and for yard facilities/managing safety equipment.
- Health and safety control on-board and for yard facilities including gas free tests.
- To provide HSSE trainings as per HSSE training manual.
- To implement and maintain ISO 9001:2008 and OHSAS 18001:2007.
- Managing occupational health in all yard facilities such dormitory and management housing.
- To provide Health & Safety trainings as per HSSE training manual.

Firefighting & Rescue Section
- Managing and operating clinic/rescue/firefighting equipment.
- To prepare company environment policy.
- Fire prevention, extinguishing, and emergency response.
- Coordination with civil Defense.

Security Section
- Managing the security policy of company.
- To carry out security tasks for protecting the yard and other assets outside of the shipyard.
- Operating guard security team.

- To issue and control passes for visitors/guest/ship-owners, meeting the security standards and requirements of IPA, ISPS codes and SOLAS.
- To co-ordinate with govt. authorities for security issues such coast guard and navy.

Environment Section
- To develop and implement environmental policies and procedures.
- To establish and maintain the environmental management system to be in line with ISO 14001/2004.
- To co-ordinate with govt. authorities for environmental issues and necessary licenses.
- To coordinate and oversee the compliance of environmental requirements.

2.6. QA/QC Department

SRM is responsible to ensure the quality standards of the repair activities on-board the ship and this section has been produced in order to introduce the QA/QC responsibilities for SRM.

Main Roles & Responsibilities
To provide necessary quality information related with quality planning & control, to conduct education of efficient and appropriate quality control, to supervise

the technical aspects, the inspection progress and quality of projects.

Quality Assurance Section
- Quality plan and company standard control.
- ISO 9000, 14000 series certifying and managing.
- To provide technical support and development in quality control.
- NDT services and control.
- To prepare different quality certificates as per business needs.

Quality Control Section
- Quality control for repair and new construction work such as steel structure, machinery, outfitting, piping, and electric work.
- Inspection, testing, and measurement report control coordinate with the ship's surveyor and representative for inspection, testing, and surveying.
- To manage re-inspection ratio of each production department.

2.7. Information Technology Department

The IT Department is provide technical support to a business or an organization's employees and train non-technical workers on the business's information systems & this section has been produced in order to introduce for SRM the IT department responsibilities.

Main Roles & Responsibilities

- To manage IT help desk and provide services to ship-owners as requested by SRM.
- To operate and maintain business information systems and hardware.
- To carry out network stabilization, QA response, security, and backup management.
- To execute IT Infrastructure investment projects and budgets.
- To operate, maintain, and improve business information systems.
- To adjust and control IT projects related with information system software.

2.8. Finance Department

A Part of the ship yard business is to manage its money & produce the yard financial statements.
This section has been produced in order to introduce the finance responsibilities for SRM.

Main Roles & Responsibilities
The Finance Department, in addition to creating strategy, directs and coordinates the company's financial planning and accounting practices. It does this to achieve company financial objectives while complying with international regulation standards, IFRS, and all laws related to finance to update related policies and procedures.

Accounts Section

- Maintenance of financial books of accounts compliant with approved Policy, procedures, and statutory laws.

- To prepare accounts to highest standards and in line with relevant IFRS and IAS.

- Production of annual/periodical management accounts.

- Recording of invoices for direct and Indirect revenues generated.

- Registering receipts and expenditure from all departments.

- Processing of payments to suppliers/service providers/others as per approved procedures.

- Processing all cash transactions.

- Compliance with financial and tax regulations.

- Satisfying the external auditors and getting the statutory audit completed within a prescribed timeframe.

- Facilitate the internal audit of financial records and data.

- Implement and utilize the IT system for Financial Accounting.

- Provide prompt information to customers, suppliers, and others.

- Reconciliation and confirmation of customer, suppliers, and other accounts.

Finance Section
- Maintain bank accounts, cash balances, periodical bank and cash reconciliations, cash management, and forecasting.

- Build up relations with local and international banks.

- Investing funds on secure deposits at best rates of return.

- Monitor financial risk and manage it to an acceptable level.

2.9. Contract & Procurement Department

SRM is responsible for tracking well the materials & service providers that required for his project repair activities.

This section has been produced in order to introduce the C&P Department responsibilities for SRM

Main Role & Responsibility

The C&P Department focuses on timely purchase of goods and services, reduces the lead time, gets involved in early discussion of projects, and establish related policy and procedures.

Contract & Procurement Section

- To set standard terms and conditions for contracts and agreements (approved by the legal department).

- To issue a contract for services and outsourcing ad set-up, mobilizing lead time.

- To find, evaluate, and register a reliable supplier in the vendor list (20% supplies should be local).

- To establish long/short term contracts for service and manpower sub-contractors in co-ordination with production.

- To submit contract, invoice, and other supporting documents to finance so as to process payments on time.

- To prepare material budget, set proper cost saving measures in each purchase of goods and services, and budget control to achieve annual cost saving targets.

- To handle the secretariat of tender committee and to provide all related supporting documents.

Logistics Section
- Transportation of materials from supplier to shipyard and customs clearance of materials (i.e. road, sea, and air freight).

- To manage taxes and invoices of materials including inspection of materials.

- Coordinate with government entities for obtaining of licenses such as import/export permits, custom duty, environmental permits, etc.

2.10. Material Management Department

The material management department   is important to the ship yard to supply of proper quality of materials is essential for ship repair projects and the avoidance of material wastage helps in controlling cost of the projects. This section has been produced in order to introduce the MM Department to SRM.

Main Roles & Responsibilities

- To manage yard warehouses, provide the materials to end user departments, maintain minimum stock level of GSI items, manage inventory ledgers, and reconcile inventory periodically.

- To maintain warehouses, sub-warehouses, and outside storage areas.

- Material control.

- Inspection and receiving materials from the supplier as per LPO and making GRN.

- To provide materials to end user department with requested lot volume and quantities for smooth operation.

- Set processes and forms for movement of inventory, such as materials.

- Transfer and issuance to a project, return of surplus materials, and transfer of material form one project to another.

- To check stock levels and issue the POR of GSI Materials.

- To use FIFO (First in First Out) method to issue materials from the warehouse.

- To manage and sell out scrap or useless materials (periodic investigation required).

- Update location of materials in ERP system.

- To manage OFE (Owner Furnished Equipment) materials.

- To manage all receiving, issuance, and consumption through ERP system.

- To optimize space utilization within and outside warehouses and minimize inventory level.

- To close project reporting as and when project is delivered.

- To close monthly reporting on all materials (direct & indirect) consumed during the month.

- Inventory reconciliation at the end of each quarter along with aging analysis, fast and slow-moving inventories.

- Liaison with the internal and external auditor for inventory reconciliation, aging analysis, etc.

- To prepare and provide consumption reports to estimators/invoicers for billing purposes before delivery of projects.

- To manage inventory ledger.

- To use ERP system to generate all above-mentioned reports.

2.11. Marketing Department

SRM will start to handle the projects after receive firm booking order from marketing department.
This section has been produced in order to introduce the marketing processes & responsibilities to SRM.

Main Roles & Responsibilities

The Marketing Department carries out sales activity, promoting, estimation of projects, and preparation of quotation, invoicing, project management for the purpose of maximizing yard business.

Planning Section

- To set marketing strategy and conduct market analysis/issuing marketing reports.
- Preparation of business expansion such as offshore repair.
- To manage external advertisement/web-site.

Marketing Section (Area Wise)

- The promotion of the yard, market development, enlargement, and strengthening.
- Contacting clients and maintaining a relationship with them.
- Determining client qualifications and credibility.
- Setting up the company's marketing policy in terms of price, discounts, credit period, quality, delivery, etc.
- Preparing and submitting offers to clients.
- Preparing offers for damaged vessels/issuing order confirmations and concluding contracts.
- Preparing pre-qualification documents.
- Settling payments and bank guarantees.
- Performing advertising, branding activities, and documentary films related to company business.

- To communicate with media for press releases, supplements, interviews, etc. ...and manage the company's corporate gifts.
- Controlling regional and international agents and preparing long term contract with them.

Estimation Section

- The reception and review of docking indents and repair/conversion specifications from clients.
- The collection of all information and data from relevant departments to prepare quotation/offer.
- Analysis of repair/conversion specification.
- Preparing quotation including work volume, quantity, time duration, and price.
- Setting the unit price of each detailed work order (tariffs) with coordination of production and concerned department.
- Analyzing the cost structure such as labor, materials, and overhead cost.
- Updating tariffs, quotations, bills, and other documents in coordination with production (same standard man-hour with estimation and production).
- To share project details with relevant department to plan for ship-repair/conversion.

2.12. Hull or Steel Department

The ship yard profit achieved mainly from the steel repairs and this lead to keep steel department on the top of the production divisions.

This section has been produced in order to introduce the steel department responsibilities to SRM.

Main Roles & Responsibilities
- Hull processing shop operating (steel processing).
- Raw steel material control (arranging, cutting, and distribution).
- Minimize wastage of raw material.
- Steel marking on curves and various shapes.
- Conversion vessel marking control.
- Hull steel structure repair.
- New steel structure processing (block fabrication/erection).

2.13. Blasting & Painting Department

The blasting and painting also is very important to the ship yard and it is the second department in the production organization, also it is profit achieves to the ship yard.

This section has been produced in order to introduce the blasting & painting department responsibilities to SRM.

Main Roles & Responsibilities
- Grit blasting or power tooling on steel structure.

- Outfitting/piping before painting.
- Painting by spray on hull steel structure or outfitting/piping.
- Touch-up carrying on paint damage parts.
- High pressure washing by water for removal of dust, rust, and salt.
- Arranging control of various paint equipment.
- Grit supplying to blasting machine.
- Ship's general cleaning/dock cleaning.
- Tank cleaning for hot work (hull, outfitting, piping, etc.).
- Tank/hold cleaning for painting (before/after).

2.14. Mechanical Department

The repairs of ship machineries & equipments it is carried out according to the running hours maintenance plan or inspection plan of classification society and at operation problem case or operation failure.   This section has been produced in order to introduce the mechanical department responsibilities to SRM.

Main Roles & Responsibilities
- M/Engine and aux. engine system overhaul, repair, and measurement.
- Aux. machinery system and cargo pump repair, and sea trial.
- Main or aux. boiler overhaul, cleaning, and repair.
- Various heat-exchanger repairs in E/R.

- Various engine parts machining in work shop.
- Boring for rudder, stern tube, and others engine parts.
- Welding, boring repair work for propulsion system.
- Steering gear and rudder system overhaul and repair/propulsion system overhaul and repair.
- Deck machinery repair/hydraulic system repair of various deck machinery.

2.15. Electrical Department

The repairs of ship electrical equipment's, automation system, instrumentation items & navigation equipment's it is carried out according to the makers maintenance plan or inspection plan of classification society and at operation problem case or operation failure.
This section has been produced in order to introduce the electrical department responsibilities to SRM.

Main Roles & Responsibilities
- Various motor and generator overhaul and repair.
- Electric panel such as M.S.B., local panel, start panel, etc.
- Power cable, lighting, switch, battery work, and sea trial.
- Radio, navigation, communication equipment repair, and calibration.
- Instrument equipment and maneuvering system calibration and repair.

2.16. Piping Department

The pipe work it is carried out for damaged pipes on the ship pipe line systems or for adding a complete new pipe line system to the existing one or modify some of pipe line.
This section has been produced in order to introduce the piping department responsibilities to SRM.

Main Roles & Responsibilities
- Ship's pipe repair (in engine room, ballast tank, cargo tank, deck, accommodation, etc.).
- New and conversion of ship's pipe processing.
- Insulation work on E/R and deck piping.

2.17. Production Control or Production Planning

Unit Department

The production control department is for monitoring the performance of yard production team & control the repair work of the sub-contractor on-board the ship.
This section has been produced in order to introduce the production control department responsibilities to SRM.

Main Roles & Responsibilities
- To publish ship repair program with docking-undocking plan.
- Load curve control for production.

- Direct and In-direct man-hour (M/H) control (Plan & Result).
- Establish measure of productivity of manpower.
- Sub-contractor control of work completion.
- Ships repair/conversion progress control.
- Provide reports of delivered/on-progress projects.

2.18. Production Support or Yard Operation Department

This department is to support the yard in it is operation & provide the ship with all general services are required. This section has been produced in order to introduce the production control department responsibilities to SRM.

Main Roles & Responsibilities

The main responsibility of the Production Support/Yard Operation Department is to ensure that the desired facilities are available at an optimum cost within safety guidelines. Additionally, it supports on time all necessary things for the production side such as all facilities, utilities, heavy transportation, production equipment, and tools.

Facility Management Section

- To control assets and do periodically preventive maintenance of facilities (super structure, buildings, etc.).
- To set preventive maintenance philosophy and manuals for all super structures and facilities.

- To develop cost saving and cost control methods; set up standards for consumption and compare them with the budget.
- Operation for plants (environmental facilities, gas plants, Air compressors, Substations).
- Operation for dock pumps and dock gates.
- Supply all utility (power, water, gas, etc.) supporting temporary utility, electric, and piping to work locations.
- Maintenance of all facilities, buildings, and civil contractures.
- Implementing different maintenance system and work orders - routine, planned, preventive, and breakdown maintenance.

Rigging & Lifting Section
- Operation for Heavy lift & Transportation equipment, jib cranes, and tower cranes.

Scaffolding Section
- Installation and dismantlement of scaffolding for all kinds of repair work.
- To manage and maintain scaffolding materials.

Dock Master Section
- Movement of ships for production.
- Arrangement of ships to dock and quay.
- Dock keel block arrangement and dock item work.

Chapter 3: Familiarization with Standard Ship Repair Specifications

This section has been produced in order to outline for ship repair managers the manner in which the technical superintendents of ship owner prepare the repair specifications.

3.1. General Services

All general services, whether in original specification or as additional, shall be verified by the owner's representative. Unauthorized general services shall not be accepted. The yard must arrange and provide all necessary services, as long as the ship is alongside or inside the dry dock, until all repair work is completed, and the ship is sailing. These services are as follows:

- Fire and Safety watchman each day.
- Garbage skips each day.
- Electrical shore power connection and disconnection.
- Electrical shore power per unit (KW).
- Temporary connection of fire main to ship's system.
- Maintaining pressure to ship's fire main each day.
- Sea circulating water (cooling line) connection.
- Sea circulating water (cooling) each day.
- Telephone connection on board ship.
- Supply of ballast water per connection.

- Supply of fresh water per connection.
- Connection and disconnection of compressed air.
- Gas-free testing per test/visit and issue of gas- free certificate.
- Electric heating lamps per connection.
- Ventilation fans and portable ducting each crane use per hour.

3.2. Hull Preparation

The charges for hull preparation works should be given in price per square meter. As soon as the dock is dry, the yard has to carry out the following:

- Remove hull fouling (scraping) immediately.
- High pressure washing (fresh water) and degreasing.
- Hull inspection by the yard, paint inspector, and ship superintendent for blasting area agreement prior to commencement of blasting.
- All ship's side valves, speed log, echo sounder, and any other external sensors are to be suitably protected prior to commencement of blasting.
- Propellers are to be protected prior to commencement of blasting.
- No application of blasting is to be made until the protections of the above mention are approved by the superintendent.
- Blasting is to be started as per an area agreement.

- Low pressure washing (fresh water) after blasting and prior to commencement of painting.
- No application of paint is to be made until hull service preparation is approved by superintendent and paint inspector.
- Technical data, such as thickness, over coating time, drying time before undocking, etc., must be adhered to.
- Application of paint will be under supervision of superintendent and paint inspector.
- Hull marking (draft marks, load line, ship names, IMO, port home, etc.).
- Paint owner supply.

Types of Hull Preparation
- Hand scraping normal
- Hand scraping hard
- Degreasing before preparation works
- High pressure jets wash
- Hydro blast
- Soda blast
- Vacuum dry blast
- Grit blast
- Grit sweep
- Grit blast to Sa 2
- Grit blast to Sa 2.5
- Spot blast to Sa 2.5
- Hose down with fresh water after dry blast
- Disc preparation to St2

Hull Painting Division Area
- Flat bottom
- Vertical sides
- Topsides

3.3. Rudder Works

As soon as the dock is dry, the ship yard has to carry out the following:

- Staging to be erected and removed after rudder works is completed.
- Rudder plug to be opened for checking of water in rudder.
- Air test is to be carried out if necessary; if any cracks are found, these are to be repaired.
- Rudder clearances are to be measured under the supervision of the ship's chief engineer.
- Handing over the report to the superintendent immediately.
- Pintels access to be removed for interior cleaning, inspection, and clearance measure.
- Repacking of stock gland (packing owner supply).
- MPI & dye check used as per superintendent instruction.
- Remove old zinc anodes and fit new ones (owner supply).

3.4. Propeller Works

As soon as the dock is dry, the yard must carry out the following:

- Staging to be erected and removed after repair work is completed.
- Rope guard to be removed and refit after repair work and testing are completed.
- Wear down to be measured in top and bottom under supervision of ship's chief engineer.
- Handing over the report to the superintendent immediately.
- Polish the propeller blades (face and back) and cover with grease.
- Propeller hub and blades dye check used as per superintendent instructions.
- Zinc anodes fitted on outer shaft seals to be checked and replaced as per superintendent instructions (owner supply).

3.5. Tail Shaft Withdrawal Works

As soon as the dock is dry, the yard has to carry out the following:

- Disconnection and removal of the propeller and landing in dock bottom.
- Disconnection and removal of tapered, keyed, and inboard tail shaft coupling.

- Drawing tail shaft outboard and landing in dock bottom for survey, cleaning, calibrating.
- Magna flux (MPI) testing of tail shaft taper and key way, refitting all on completion.
- Disconnection of inboard intermediate shaft, flanged couplings, releasing one in number journal bearing holding down bolts.
- Rigging intermediate shaft, lifting clear, and placing in temporary storage on ship's side, withdrawing tail shaft inboard.
- Hanging in accessible position, cleaning, calibrating, and refitting on completion.
- Relocating intermediate shaft and journal bearing in original position, fitting all holding-down bolts and recoupling flanges - all done as before.

3.6. Tail Shaft Simplex Seals Works

As soon as the dock is dry, the yard must carry out the following:

- Disconnection and removal of forward and aft seal liners.
- Removing ashore to workshop.
- Fully opening it up.
- Cleaning for examination and calibration.
- Reassembling with new rubber seals from owner's supply.
- Excluding all machining works.

3.7. Cathodic Protection Works

As soon as the dock is dry, the yard must carry out the following:

- Cut off existing anodes as per superintendent instructions.
- Refit the new anodes (owner supply) as per owner marking the locations.
- Protect any anodes prior to commencement of painting.
- Anodes protection to be removed after painting is completed.

3.8. Sea Chests Works

As soon as the dock is dry, the yard must carry out the following:

- Staging to be erected and removed after work required is completed.
- Sea chest grids to be opened for cleaning and washing.
- Blasting as per an area agreement.
- Painting as per paint maker instructions and as approved by superintendent.
- Cut off existing zinc anodes as per superintendent instructions.
- New zinc anodes to be fitted (owner supply).

- Zinc anodes to be protected prior to commencement of painting.
- Zinc anodes protection to be removed after superintendent approval.
- Sea chest grids to be closed after completion.

3.9. Bottom Plugs

As soon as the dock is dry and when directed by the superintendent, the yard must carry out the following:

- Bottom plugs to be opened and checked as marked by ship's staff.
- Any plug needing renewal must be renewed through a new job order.
- Any block needing shifting to enable the opening of the plug must be done through a new job order.
- Bottom plugs are to be closed and tested after completion.

3.10. Sea & Side Storm Valves Works

The yard must carry out the following:

- Valves to be opened in situ as marked and listed by ship's chief engineer.
- Valves to be cleaned, lapped, repacked, and painted.

- Valves spindle, gland, disk, and other items to be checked.
- Valves to be inspected by superintendent and ship's chief engineer.
- Valves to be closed after superintendent approval.
- Any fabrications or spars supply must be done through a new job order.
- Any valve needing to be completely overhauled in the workshop must be done through a new job order.

3.11. Fenders Repairs

As soon as the dock is dry, the yard must carry out the following:

- Staging to be erected and removed after repair work is completed.
- Marking of damaged fender to be carried out in presence of ship's superintendent.
- Cropping existing damaged fender, hand grinding remaining edges, and preparing remaining flat hull plating for welding.
- Supply and fit new fender in half-round standard schedule 80 steel pipe with full fillet welding fender in place.
- Paint to be applied.

3.12. Bilge Keel Repairs

As soon as the dock is dry, the yard must carry out the following:

- Staging to be erected and removed after repair work is completed.
- Marking of damaged bilge keel to be carried out in presence of ship's superintendent.
- Cropping existing damaged bilge keel, hand grinding remaining edges and preparing remaining flat hull plating for welding.
- Supply and fit new bilge keel and weld in place.
- Paint to be applied.

3.13. Anchors & Chains Works

As soon as the dock is dry, the yard must carry out the following:

- Anchor chains (P&S) are to be lowered and ranged in dock bottom.
- Both chains are to be washed and cleaned.
- Both chains are to be calibrated and a report handed over to the superintendent.
- Both chains are to be joined end to end.
- Both chains studs are to be inspected.
- Mark all shots with paint and wires.
- After confirming anchor swivel and pin are free, lift up prior to undocking.

3.14. Chain Lockers Works

As soon as the anchor chains are ranged in dock bottom, the ship yard must carry out the following:

- Both chain lockers manholes are to be opened.
- Both chain lockers are to be cleaned and have mud removed.
- Both chain lockers are to be washed; pump out washing water after washing.
- Superintendent inspection.
- Both chain lockers are to be painted as per superintendent's instruction.
- Manhole is to be closed after superintendent approval.

3.15. Steel Repairs

Marking off the damaged area of hull plating is to be carried out according to UTG drawings in the presence of ship's superintendent:

- Cropping by hand burning and removal of all cropped plating.
- Dressing and preparation of plate edges of remaining external plating.
- Dressing and preparation of remaining internal structure.

- Supply and preparation of new steel plating, blasting to Sa2.5 and applying one coat of holding primer.
- Transport of new plate to vessel, fitting up, wedging in position, minor fairing and dressing of plate edges in the immediate vicinity, applying first runs of welding on one side, back gouging from other side and finally filling and capping to give fully finished weld.
- NDT to be carried out.

3.16. Pipe Works

According to listed pipes by C/E, the yard must carry out the following:
- Removal of existing pipe and disposal ashore.
- Fabrication of new pipe in workshop to pattern of existing one complete with new flanges.
- Pipe pressure test to be carried out.
- Delivery on board of new pipe and installation in place with supply of new jointing, bolts, and nuts.
- Refit of original clamps with new bolts and nuts.

3.17. Mechanical Works

3.17.1. Main Engine - Piston Withdrawal

According to engine running hours record & class inspection plan, the yard must carry out the following:
- Open up cylinder cover.
- Remove piston.
- Clean under scavenging space, smoothen cylinder liner in way of ports and collar.
- Test cylinder L.O. System by hand operating.
- Renew piston rings (owners supply) and smoothen up rings edges.
- Check piston top clearances by ships gauge and record readings.

3.17.2. Main Engine - Cylinder Liner Withdrawal

According to engine running hours record & class inspection plan, the yard must carry out the following:
- Withdraw liner, clean, and paint cooling surface.
- Replace with new rings (owners supply) and carry out pressure test.

Extra Jobs:
1. Removal of jacket.
2. Transportation to work shop.
3. Lapping and machining of landing surface.

3.17.3. Main Engine – Start Air Valves and Safety Valve

According to class inspection plan, the yard must carry out the following:
- Disconnect valve.
- Open up.
- Clean.
- Grind in.
- Inspection and adjustment on completion.

3.17.4. Main Engine – Fuel Oil Injection Valve

- Disconnect valve.
- Open up.
- Clean and grind in contact surface; carry out pressure test.

3.17.5. Main Engine Stuffing Box

According to engine running hours record & class inspection plan, the yard must carry out the following:
- Remove stuffing box to workshop.
- Open up, skim, and face up contact surfaces.
- Adjust gap or renew rings (owners supply).

3.17.6. Main Engine Bearing Inspection

According to engine running hours record & class inspection plan, the yard must carry out the following:
- Open up upper half.
- Clean, inspect, and check.
- Record clearances.

- Close up on completion.

3.17.7. Cross Head and Bottom End Bearing Inspection

According to engine running hours record & class inspection plan, the yard must carry out the following:
- Open up bearing for inspection of lower and upper halves.
- Clean, check, and record clearances.
- Close up on completion.

3.17.8. Main Thrust Bearing

According to engine running hours record & class inspection plan, the yard must carry out the following:
- Open up upper half, draw out pads, clean and inspect.
- Measure thrust and journal bearing clearances with feller gauge.
- Close up on completion.

3.17.9. Crankcase Cleaning

According to class inspection plan, the yard must carry out the following:
- Open up crankcase doors.
- Superintendent inspection.
- Clean crankcase and close up on completion.

3.17.10. Main Engine Crank Shaft Deflection

- Measure and record engine deflection afloat condition before entering dry dock and after un-docking.

3.17.11. Turbo Chargers Overhauling

According to engine running hours record & class inspection plan, the yard must carry out the following:
- Open up turbo chargers and clean all parts thoroughly.
- Measure and record clearances of the bearing and rotor shaft.
- Replace worn out parts (owners supply).
- Rotor balancing test.
- Reassemble and refit in good order.

3.17.12. Air Coolers

The yard must carry out the following:
- Disconnect and remove cooler.
- Clean sea water and air side with chemicals.
- Paint covers and water box.
- Renew zinc anodes (owners supply).
- Hydro test.
- Reassemble.

3.17.13. Heat Exchangers

The yard must carry out the following:
- Open up covers.

- Clean sea water side, water box, and cover interiors.
- Paint with one coat and renew zinc anodes (owners supply).
- Chemical cleaning.
- Hydro test.

3.17.14. Main Condenser
The yard must carry out the following:
- Open up manhole covers on both ends.
- Clean water box and tube plates.
- Blow clear tubes and renew zinc anodes (owners supply).
- Chemical cleaning.
- Hydro test.

3.17.15. Fire Tube Boiler Cleaning

According to class inspection plan, the yard must carry out the following:
- Remove access doors.
- Clean fire and water sides with fresh water.
- Survey and close after inspection.

The following are excluded:
- Hard scrapping or chipping of heavy deposits.
- Cleaning of air heaters.
- Opening of hand hole doors.
- Chemical cleaning.
- Hydro testing.

- Any repairs and renewals.
- Gaskets (owners supply).

3.17.16. Water Tube Boiler Cleaning

According to class inspection plan, the yard must carry out the following:
- Open access doors for cleaning and wash down fire sides with fresh water.
- Open steam water drum doors, head clean drums, and close after inspection.

The following are excluded:
- Hard scrapping or chipping of heavy deposits.
- Cleaning of air heaters.
- Opening of hand hole doors.
- Chemical cleaning.
- Hydro testing.
- Any repairs and renewals.
- Gaskets (owners supply).

3.17.17. Main Steam Turbine

According to the operation manual instruction class inspection plan, the yard must carry out the following:
- Disconnect steam pipe and insulation.
- Install ships lifting tool.
- Open and lift upper casing for examination/survey.
- Measure labyrinth clearance and close on completion.

The following are excluded:
- Insulation.
- Adjusting the labyrinth.
- Repair and renewals.
- Opening of control gear.

3.17.18. Main Steam Turbine Bearing

According to the operation manual instruction class inspection plan, the yard must carry out the following:
- Open up, clean, and examine forward and aft journal and thrust bearing.
- Measure, clearance, and close on completion.

3.17.19. Main Steam Turbine Flexible Coupling

According to the operation manual instruction class inspection plan, the yard must carry out the following:
- Open up coupling for cleaning and examination.
- Survey, measure, and record clearances.
- Close on completion.

The following are excluded:
- Checking and adjustment alignment.
- Repair and renewals.

3.17.20. Alternator Turbine - Turbine Side

According to the operation manual instruction class inspection plan, the yard must carry out the following:

- Disconnect steam pipes for access.
- Open up casing, rotor bearing, and coupling.
- Lift up rotor using ships lifting tool.
- Check labyrinth.
- Measure bearing clearances.
- Check rotor with dial gauge.
- Close on completion.

3.17.21. Alternator Turbine - Reduction Gear

According to the operation manual instruction class inspection plan, the yard must carry out the following:
- Open up casing pinion, and gear bearing top halves.
- Clean and check back lash of gears.
- Measure clearances and close on completion.

3.17.22. Compressors Overhauling
The yard must carry out the following:
- Open up cylinders covers and crank pin bearing.
- Draw pistons.
- Renew ring, if necessary (owners supply).
- Remove piston pins.
- Open up main bearings.
- Clean and face up suction and delivery valves for inspection.
- Cleaning of air cooler to be included.

3.17.23. Air Bottles

The yard must carry out the following:

- Open up manholes.
- Clean and wipe dry interior for inspection.
- On completion, paint owners supply air bottle.
- Refit manholes with new gaskets.

3.17.24. Ship System Valves Overhauling

According to listed valves by C/E, the yard must carry out the following:
- Opening up listed globe and gate valve for in situ overhaul.
- Disconnecting and removing cover, spindle and gland, cleaning all exposed parts, hand grinding of globe valve, light hand scraping of gate valve.
- Testing bedding in presence of ship's superintendent.
- Paint internal exposed areas and reassembling with new cover joint and repacking gland.

3.17.25. Oil tanker Cargo Pumps Overhauling

According to the operation manual instruction class inspection plan, the yard must carry out the following:
- Disconnecting and removing top half of casing.
- Releasing shaft flexible coupling from drive.
- Slinging and removing impeller, shaft and wearing rings.
- Withdraw impeller, shaft sleeve, and bearings from shaft.
- Cleaning all exposed parts, calibrating, and reporting.

- Reassembling as before using owner's supplied parts.
- Operation test in presence of ship's superintendent.

3.17.26. Ship System Pumps (centrifugal-type) Overhauling

As per ship technical superintendent instruction, the yard must carry out the following:
- Disconnecting and removing top half of casing.
- Release shaft coupling from motor drive.
- Slinging and removing impeller, shaft, and wearing rings.
- Withdraw impeller, shaft sleeve, and bearings from shaft.
- Cleaning all exposed parts, calibrating and reporting.
- Reassembly as before using owners supplied parts.
- Operation test in presence of ship's superintendent.

3.17.27. Ship System Pumps (reciprocating-type pumps, steam driven) Overhauling

As per ship technical superintendent instruction, the yard must carry out the following:
- Disconnecting and removing steam cylinder top cover.
- Release steam piston, withdrawing, removing piston rings.

- Clean, calibrate, and recording.
- Disconnecting and removing slide valve cover.
- Removing valves, cleaning, and presenting for survey.
- Disconnecting and removing bucket cover.
- Release bucket, withdrawing, removing bucket rings.
- Clean, calibrate, and recording.
- Opening up suction and delivery valve chest.
- Remove the valves and springs.
- Cleaning, grinding, and presenting for survey.
- Fully reassemble complete pump, renewing all jointing and repacking glands with owner's supplied.
- Operation test in presence of ship's superintendent.

3.17.28. Ship System Pumps (reciprocating-type pumps, electric motor driven) Overhauling

As per ship technical superintendent instruction, the yard must carry out the following:
- Disconnecting, removing electric motor, and putting it aside.
- Disconnecting and removing bucket cover.
- Releasing bucket, with-drawing, removing bucket rings.
- Cleaning, calibrating, and recording.
- Opening up suction and delivery valve chest.
- Removing valves and springs, cleaning, grinding, and presenting for survey.

- Fully reassemble complete pump, renewing all jointing and repacking glands with owner's supplied.
- Reinstalling electric motor and making terminals.
- Operation test in presence of ship's superintendent.

3.17.29. Steering Pump Overhauling

As per ship technical superintendent instruction, the yard must carry out the following:
- Disconnecting pump and removing for in situ overhaul.
- Open up pump, full dismantling, cleaning calibrating and presenting for survey.
- Fully reassemble using owner's supplied spares and reinstalling in place.

3.17.30. Gear Pump Overhauling

As per ship technical superintendent instruction, the yard must carry out the following:
- Disconnecting and removing pump, opening up end covers, withdrawing gear units, cleaning, calibrating, recording clearances, and presenting them for survey.
- Fully reassemble pump, renewing all jointing and repacking glands with owner's supplied packing or seals.

3.18. Electrical Works

3.18.1. Switchboard Cleaning

As per ship technical superintendent instruction &the item for class inspection, the yard must carry out the following:
- Cleaning behind switchboard.
- Examining all connections and retightening as necessary.
- Reporting conditions.

3.18.2. Electrical Motors Overhauling

As per ship technical superintendent instruction & according to motor repair list, the yard must carry out the following:
- Disconnecting motor from location.
- Transporting motor ashore to workshop for rewinding.
- Receiving motor in workshop, dismantling, cutting out all stator coils, removing rotor bearings, and cleaning all parts.
- Forming new stator coils in copper wire assembling, using new insulation and varnish.
- Baking dry in oven, dip varnishing and re-baking in oven. Reassembling all parts, fitting new standard

type ball or roller bearings to rotor and testing in workshop.
- Returning motor back on board and refitting in original position and reconnecting original cables.
- Final operation test on-board in presence of ship's superintendent.

3.18.3. Electric Generators (alternators) Overhauling

According to ship technical superintendent instruction & class plan for inspection, the yard must carry out the following:
- Disconnecting and removing rotor ashore to workshop.
- Full cleaning, baking in oven, drying, varnishing, and re-baking in oven.
- Work shop testing in presence of ship's superintendent.
- Return it back on-board.
- Reassembling and reconnecting in place on board.
- Alignment to be carried out and reported.
- Operation test on-board in presence of ship's superintendent.

Chapter 4: Familiarization with the Project Management Procedures

This chapter has been produced in order to introduce to SRM in details the project management include SRM responsibilities and the project management processes from marketing stage to ship delivery stage.

4.1. Ship Repair Manager Duties & Responsibilities

- Compilation of all information available from commercial file in order to prepare all standard documents necessary for the work and distribution to yard services concerned.
- Clarifications with customer representative of any unclear item in the customer specification resulting from detailed discussions with yard services.
- Board the vessel on way for inspection and reporting on arrival.
- Clarification and agreement with customer representative of required condition for the vessel on arrival as well as requirements for docking,

taking into consideration specifications and yard procedures.

- Enquiry for availability of any technical information necessary for the works (drawing, specification, owner's decision on spare parts, etc.).
- Discussion and agreement with yard's services of the work preliminary schedule.
- Meeting with customer representative and staff on arrival, introducing them to the yard's normal practice safety regulations and procedures,
- Identification on site of specified works with the services concerned and agreement on technical aspects according to the yard's practice and capabilities.
- Follow-up works in progress and schedule of repairs, identifying deviations, processing eventual corrective measures to minimize idle time, maintain delivery dates, and optimizing the use of yard facilities/equipment.
- Attendance of meetings with customer representative and staff for discussion of all pertinent aspects of work, in particular, process variations of work and their effects on the schedule.
- Safety aspects and interference between the yard and customers staff work requirements for customer supplied items.
- Eventual receipt of complaints addressing the same to concerned yard services and, if required,

process the same as per yard quality assurance system.

- Preparation of change orders and assistance on provision of details to sales department to allow preparation of quotations.
- Assurance that quality of work is commercially acceptable according to established procedures and obtain approval for work completed from customer representative.
- Attendance of production meetings to report on progress of work and relevant problems related with project.
- Maintenance of close and daily contacts with the yard's safety officers and the yard's services; initiate meeting, when required, with them and customer staff to agree on procedures, sequence, priorities of conflicting tasks, unsafe conditions, and measures to be taken to minimize any negative effect on the schedule.

4.2. Ship Repair Project Management Processes

SRM must know the project processes from ship pre-arrival to the ship deliver & that to allow him for more controls on the project from the day he receives his nominated letter to ship deliver day.

4.2.1 Pre-Arrival Ship Processes

Communication with Ship Owners:

- Marketing contacting clients and maintain relationships with themes using basic communication skills to build strong relationships with ship owners by local and overseas ship agent, face to face meetings, visit & attend all International Maritime Exhibitions, E-mails exchanges, arrange annual gathering day for ship owners, phone calls, upgrading yard website, plan for annual business trip travel, etc.

- Receive and review of docking intentions and repair specification from the clients for quotation purpose, marketing in-charge is required to review the repair specification and assure that it has full required information for estimation calculation such as ship particulars, ship drawings, steel dimensions or quantity, pipe length and diameters, tanks size and volume, blasting and painting area, engines details, propellers dimensions, etc. and any others technical data and drawings can help estimation department in the estimation process, otherwise he should return back directly to the requesters in order to clear with themes all unclear items in the repair specification.

- Once the repair specification is completed it will be forwarded to the estimation department for estimation process.

Quotation Process:

- Estimation Department receives the full repair specification from the yard marketing team for preparing the quotations according to yard tariffs while analyzing the cost structure of the projects such as labors, materials, subcontractors or service engineer's arrangement and overhead cost.

- Estimators prepare the quotation of the repair specification activities, arrange, and list the quotation items with attaching ship yard main facilities information's such as:

1. Repair berths numbers, drafts, and lengths.
2. Dry dock numbers, dead weight capacities, minimum depth of water, length and width.
3. Floating dock numbers, dock lifting capacity, length, width, dock cranes and crane lifting capacity.
4. Yard cranes numbers, cranes location, lifting capacity for each and maximum outreach for each.
5. Floating cranes numbers and the lifting capacity for each.
6. Tug boat numbers and bollard pull capacity for each.

Quotation general remarks such as:

1. All prices quote is in USD and are subject to variation due to changes in cost and availability of material.
2. All prices quoted for repairs carried out in our yard premises.
3. All prices are based on work being carried out during normal working hours.
4. All prices are quoted unless mentioned in the tariff excluding removals for access, staging, cleaning, rust freeing, testing, painting, ventilation, and lighting.
5. All work to be carried out as per yard general terms, conditions, and yard safety regulations.
6. Yard working hours and official holidays.

- After the yard estimators have completed the price list of the repair specification, the marketing person in-charge will review it once more. Then. he should return it back to the yard estimators for any miscalculation, missing items or unclear items until setting up the full correct price list.

- Next, he has to arrange and send to the ship owner's the yard tender which consists of the quotation covering (price list), yard terms and conditions, dry dock firm booking, repair schedule, and ship delivery.

- Here, the negotiation exchanges will start between ship owner and yard marketing around the yard price wise, docking period, delivery date and/or various items on yard terms and conditions.

- After the yard marketing in-charge person has fixed all the negotiated points with ship owners according to yard top management instructions, he must prepare the final tender agreement for approvals from yard managers and ship owner - owner will revert back to the yard with his confirmation for firm booking and tender.

- Marketing in-charge person will reply to the ship owner with yard acceptance firm booking then issuing the orders confirmation with identification code.

- Distribute this order to all concerned departments such as estimation, SRM, production, procurement, invoicing, etc.

Preparing the Project Commercial File

It is very important that the marketing in-charge person integrates hard copies of the project information, specification, quotation, term and condition, correspondences, owner firm booking confirmation, yard firm booking acceptance, etc. He must keep it in one file to be as reference for reviewing by everyone that has related work to the project and useful guides of the next process.

Nomination of Ship Repair Manager for the Project

The head of ship repair management department will nominate the project ship repair manager to coordinate repair activities and hand over a copy of the project commercial file to the SRM. This is done to study all information available from commercial file for preparing all standard documents necessary for the work (repair plan, activity code, etc.) and distribution to yard services concerned.

Accordingly, the SRM will conduct a pre-arrival meeting with the yard concerning department in-charges to make sure that:

1. All technical information and drawings are available and clear for them.
2. Each concern department has been issued the POR of required material supply, spare parts supply (if by yard), services engineers arrangement and subcontractors manpower supply.
3. The fabrications (if any) have been started according to owner work specification.
4. Design or technical section has received all required ship drawings for keel block arrangement

such as docking plan, general arrangement, mid-ship section, and shell expansion.

5. Dock master has received and accepted the ship ballast condition.
6. All required general services (shore power, telephone connection, cooling water, etc.) are available upon request.

- After the pre-arrival meeting with yard team the SRM will send an e-mail to the ship owner for the following:

1. Introduce himself and provide his contact details.
2. Clarify with customer representative of any unclear items or unavailable drawings in customer specifications resulting from detailed discussions with concerned yard departments during pre-arrival meeting.
3. Data required prior to arrival such as updated ETA, Superintendent's full contact details, Vessel's local agent's details, Vessel's armory status/clearance? If so, confirm agent's preparations/proceedings with local authorities.

4.2.2 After Ship Arrival

SRM Arrangement for Kick Off & Safety Meeting:
- This meeting should take place on the first working day after ship arrival at the yard. The ship repair manager should start the meeting by introducing

himself as the yard in-charge person for the repairs. Additionally, he should give his telephone number to the owner's representative, showing him he can be easily contacted during office hours or overnight in case of emergency.

- The ship repair manager should then introduce yard in-charge personnel attending the meeting starting with the yard safety officer.

- The yard safety officer would then give a short description for yard safety rules and highlight the on-board safety procedures in particular.

- The ship repair manager must mention clearly that all orders have to be channeled through him only to avoid misunderstanding and to ensure that the order has been passed to the right department in the yard.

- The ship repair manager has to agree with the superintendent on a suitable time for daily on-board meetings.

Works Identification

Identification on site of specified works with the concerned department and agreement on technical aspects according to the yards practice and capabilities.

Daily Meeting On-Board

During this meeting, the ship repair manager briefs the superintendent and ship crew on the progress of repair highlighting the difficulties, if any, due to shortage of spares, lateness of decision, or unclear identification of various items.

All change orders should be discussed with the superintendent during this meeting before issuing them to production departments.

Ship Repair Division Management Meeting

The ship repair manager has to report directly to the SRM senior manager and it should be as short as possible using the ship repair plan to highlight any delay which might affect completion of the repair - be specific.

Communication with Yard Departments:

- It is very important to have your own inspection early in the morning onboard the ship and in the yard workshop.
- Give your instructions directly to the in-charge person clear and be specific.
- Avoid as much as you can using the radio and phone to discuss or solve problems with an in-charge person; it should be face to face.

- On completion of any items make your own inspection with the in-charge person and Q.C. before calling the superintendent or ship crew for final inspection.

Initiate the Change Order with Owner Approval

It is very important to prepare the change order to cover any deviation from the original specification (additional or cancelation) as soon as possible to avoid any misunderstanding, especially if this change will affect the completion date of subject repair.

Ship Dock in Follow-Up:
- Request from the ship master the ship ballast condition with zero list and review it with concerned yard departments for approval.
- Check with the dock master about the keel block arrangement progress.
- Confirm with the ship master the yard docking plan (date and time).
- Confirm with the ship master the ship machinery conditions such as mooring winches, generators, ship cranes, ballast pump, etc.
- Follow up with yard pilot the entering progress.
- Confirm with the ship master that the ship has received all required services inside the dock such as electrical shore connection, cooling connection, gangway, etc.

Work Follow-Up During Repair Period

Follow-up work in progress and schedule of repairs, identifying any deviations while processing eventual corrective measures to minimize idle time; maintain delivery dates and optimize the use of yard facilities/equipment.

Focusing on the Critical Items:
- Steel work progress, especially inside the tanks.
- Blasting and painting progress, especially tank treatment.
- Spare parts supply or service arrangement by owner to be followed up at every meeting.
- Spare parts supply or service arrangement by yard to be followed up with yard procurement at every moment.
- Tested items such as load test, MPI, etc. should be considered priority and expect test failure to affect the project's progress.
- Class item can affect repair progress because of class surveyor's notifications and remarks.
- Items on-hold by the owner are to be followed up with him at every meeting.
- Additional works to be started immediately unless there are no spares or materials are needed for supply.
- Ship undocking follow-up procedure.
- Receive ballast condition from ship's captain for yard dock master's approval.

- Ensure that the ship has received all the ballast water quantities required for undocking the ship safely.

Check that all Under Water Items (undocking items) Have Been Done (not limited to the below mentioned):

- Sea valves and filters are tightened in place.
- Bottom plugs are tightened in place and tested with vacuum tester.
- Hull-painting, touch up, and marking has been completed.
- Steel repair under water has been completed, tested, and approved by class.
- Sea chest has been closed after owner inspection and approval.
- Ballast valves are tightened in place.
- Lift up anchor and chains.
- Rudder and propellers are in place.
- Echo sounder and speed log has been tested with vacuum tester.
- Any other items that can be effect on ship undocking.

Un-Docking Follow-Up Procedure:
- Ensure that all in-charge persons and their workers required for ship undocking are available on-board during the start of filling water in the dock.

- Agree with yard dock master that before the ship becomes afloat to stop filling water so as to check with in-charge person concerning any water leakage inside the engine room, pump room, etc.

- In case there is water leakage, the ship repair manager must directly contact the dock master to inform him; never start continuous filling of water till receiving ship repair manager's final confirmation.

- Once the ship becomes afloat with no leakage, the ship repair manager has to ask the chief engineer to start up the ship's generator.

- After ship generator is running, the ship repair manager has to give the order to the utility in-charge person to disconnect shore power.

- The ship repair manager will leave the ship after he is sure that all yard personnel are on shore.

Sea Trial Follow-Up Procedure:

- Sea trial will be carried out by ship crew and ship yard personnel to check the condition of main engine and anything attached to it (governor, turbocharger, etc.).

- The ship repair manager will attend the trial to coordinate between the yard in-charge person and make sure that the ship is ready for delivery without any problems.

Work Completion Reports Follow-Up for Invoicing

The ship repair manager will coordinate between yard production departments, to get feedback on the work completion report, and the invoicers/estimators for final invoicing process before ship departure.

Invoicer/Estimator Final Negotiation

Attend the final bill negotiation with the ship repair estimator and ship technical superintendent to confirm that all items have been carried out by the yard are covered in the final bill, without any doubt between the ship owner and yard estimator.

Chapter 5: Familiarization with the Form in Use Related to Projects

5.1. Change Orders Form

CHANGE ORDER / WORK START ORDER

PROJECT			ORDER NO.	DATE	CHANGE ORDER NO.
	0		0		

ACTIVITY CODE	OWNER SPEC. NO.	JOB DESCRIPTION			

DETAILED DESCRIPTION :		REQUIREMENTS
		Lighting
		Ventilation
		Staging
		Cleaning for Access
		Access Work
		Grit Blasting
		Painting
		Material Yard Supply
		Material Owner Supply
		Transport to Workshop
		Testing before
		Testing after
		DEPARTMENT
		Hull
		Mechanical
		Outfitting
		Elect.
		Pro. Sup.
		QC
		Stagers
		Blasting & Painting

Work Start Approval :

Note :   When used a Work Start Order, only signature of Ship Manager required.

COMMENTS:

	Owner Request Qutation Frist?	YES	NO

Ship Repair Manager   Customer Representative

- This form is used when the project has work variation from the original repair specification or new additional job, also it can be used for work cancelation.
- It should include all clear technical information such as:
1. Material specification.
2. The quantity, Length X wide X Dia.
3. Equipment makers and serial No.
4. Type of services like overhauling or overhauling, etc.

5.2. Services & Safety Requirements Form

SERVICES / SAFETY REQUIREMENTS

VESSEL NAME	:	0		SHIP REPAIR MANAGER :	0
ORDER NO.	:	0		MOB TEL NO. :	
E.T.A.	:		APT _ _ ER	EPT	DATE OF ISSUE :
ARRIVAL DRAFT	:				BERTH NO. :
FWD	:				DOCK NO. :
AFT	:			BOW IN [ ]	STERN IN [ ]

Item NO.	ITEM	LOCATION	PROVIDED BY		DONE ON		Owner Confirmation
			Name	Signture	Date	Time	
	I.G. GENERATOR						
	LIGHTS/VENTS						
	EXTRACTORS						
	HOT WORK LOCATIONS						
	INERTED TKS						
	BALLASTED TKS						
	Feir Line						
	Cooling Line						

| In-Charge Engineer: | Sign.: |

On Completion Return Back To Ship Repair Manager:

- This form is used before ship arrival at the yard and is prepared by the SRM with all general services required for the project.
- Hand it over to the services department in order to arrange services upon ship arrival at yard.
- Return it back to the SRM with ship master's confirmation of services receipt.

5.3. Ballast & De-ballast Request Form

BALLAST / DEBALLAST REQUIREMENTS

TO: Production Support	TO BE COMPLETED BY Production Support SERVICE AND RETURNED TO SHIP REPAIR MANAGER ON COMPLETION
SHIP'S NAME: 0 ORD.# 0 JOB #	
EXPECTED TO START ON: AT HOURS	ACTUAL DATE STARTED : COMPLETED :

S.N.:	TANK NO.	QUANTITY (M.T.)	TO BE FILLED-UP THRU : (HATCH, MANIFOLD etc.)	TIME START	STOP	TIME START	STOP	TOTAL HOURS SPENT (NET)	REMARKS
TOTAL									

HOSE ARRANGEMENT

AFT   A.P.T.   E.R.   P.R.   E.P.T.   FWD

SHIP REPAIR MANAGER: 0	
DATE OF ISSUE:	Utility IN-CHARGE: / EMP.NO.

- This form is used when the SRM receives the ballast condition from the ship master.
- Hand it over to the concerned department for arranging all the required accordingly.
- Return it back to the SRM upon operation completion with ship master's confirmation of receipt of all ballast quantities.

5.4. Services to Be Carried Out By Owner

SERVICES TO BE CARRIED OUT ON BOARD
ON DIRECT ORDER BY CUSTOMER

Project		Order	
		Date	

The services described below were ordered directly by Owners. The Yard is requested to allow free access to Yard and vessel to the below identified contractor to perform described services.

Service Description: _____

_____

_____

_____

_____

Contractor : _____

_____

_____

Expected Starting Date: _____ **Duration:** _____

_____   _____
Ship Repair Manager   **Customer Representative**
(Name & Signature)   (Name & Signature)

Note :
According to Yard's Rules, the above is agreed on condition of acceptance of Yards Safety Rules and Regulations by Owners' Representative and Contractor.
Performed services should not interfere with Yard's schedule.
Any assistance required from Yard shall

istribution: Original in duplicate for Owners & Commercial File; Procurement Service; Safety Service; Security Servi

- According to yard policy, it is not allowed for the ship owner to carry out any services on-board during the repair period unless allowed by the ship yard.
- The SRM is to issue this form after getting his manager's confirmation.

5.5. Ship Equipment/Materials Off- Loading Form

<table>
<tr><td colspan="4" align="center">EQUIPMENT / MATERIALS OFFLOADING</td></tr>
<tr><td>Project</td><td></td><td>Order</td><td></td></tr>
<tr><td>IMO No.</td><td></td><td></td><td></td></tr>
<tr><td>Customer</td><td></td><td>Date</td><td></td></tr>
</table>

The item(s) described below was offloaded in the Yard as per instructions received:

1. Item Description:

2. Reason for Offloading:

- ☐ To be used on _____
- ☐ To be exported to _____.
- ☐ Awaiting instructions from Owners.
- ☐ Scrap.
- ☐ Other Reasons.

3. Identification Marks:

4. Location for Storage:

5. Remarks:

Ship Repair Manager	Customer Representative
(Name & Signature)	(Name & Signature)

Note:
According to Yard's Rules, above described item(s) will be stored for a maximum period of 6 (six) months unless otherwise agreed in writing by Yard's Commercial Division.
After above period expires, Yard reserves the right to dispose off the item(s) as found convenient, without further notice or compensation to Owners.
During the storage period Yard's General Terms and Conditions will be applicable.

Distribution: Original in duplicate for Owners & Commercial File; Security Service; Warehouse; Ship Repair Office

- Sometimes, during the repair period, ship owners make a request to the ship yard for off-loading certain equipment or materials for various reasons until ship repair is completed. Also, this form is used for scarp disposal.

- It is very important for the SRM use it in order to avoid any misunderstandings at the end of the project.

5.6. Exemption of Liability

Mr. ....
Customer Representative
Vessel ....
At (Yard Name)

Dear Sir,

Sub. : Vessel ....

Reference is made to the repairs being performed on item .....

For the sake of good record, according to a note received from our Production Services, we hereby confirm that repairs will be/were carried out according to instructions received and bring to your notice the following:

-
-
-
-
-
-
-

We shall appreciate your comments on the above, if deemed necessary.

Thanking you,

Yours faithfully,

Ship Repair Manager

This form is issued by the SRM after receiving the condition report from the concerned department. It includes technical remarks indicating if the equipment is good or beyond repair; hand it over to the ship owner for decision making.

Chapter 6: How to Build Your Experiences as a Ship Repair Manager

Always keep in your mind that "Problems are experiences". No experiences can be gained, or growth can occur until you face project problems and share the proper solution of them.

However, some advice can help you at the beginning to become a professional SRM.

6.1. Read the Repair Specifications Carefully Before Ship Arrival

For each and every project, read the repair specifications several times, focus on the technical information, write down your comments and questions, mark un-clear items for discussion with the ship owner, and initiate a draft plan for the project according to available information.

6.2. Stay Very Close with Your Oldest Colleagues

Hear them and learn from them. Focus on their discussion during SRM department meetings. Visit their projects and attend their meetings on-board. Lastly, see what they are talking about and discussing with ship owners and the yard team.

6.3. Record Daily Events

Daily, you must write down the major events of the project such as: technical issues, work progress delays, any advice you have received, project problems, IT solutions, etc.

6.4. Learning Target for Each Project

For example, you have received a nomination letter from your department head with the repair specifications. You read it well and indicate select certain items as learning targets of the practical technical process such as tail shaft withdrawal. Once the ship enters the dry dock, you should start monitoring the tail shaft progress from staging erection until shaft reassembly while recording every and each step.

This must be repeated at every project with different activities.

6.5. Spend Almost All Your Time On-board & in the Work Shop

Experiences will not be gained inside your office. Project problems will never be solved by phone calls alone. A ship repair career is not simply administration duties but involves practical hard work. So, if you are not on the work location, you will quickly lose project control.

6.6. Build a Good Relationship with the Ship Technical Superintendent

The ship technical superintendent is supposed to be the most experienced person on-board the ship. You would benefit from building a good relationship with him, exchanging with him technical discussions about the project.

6.7. Build a Good Relationship with Class Surveyors

Try to attend the class surveyor's inspection on-board and inside the workshops; record his remarks for a discussion with him later.

6.8. Build a Good Relationship with the Service Engineers

Whenever you have service engineers on-board, you should attend their meetings with ship owners; visit them on work location and record what you have heard and seen for discussion with them.

Chapter 7: Ship Crew Duties Prior to Entering the Drydock

This chapter has been produced in order to introduce to SRM the ship crew responsibilities on-board the ship prior entering the dry dock.

7.1. General

- The master is to ensure that a plan for the intended passage of a vessel is prepared before sailing.

- It is particularly important that this procedure is adopted both for the voyage in coastal waters (restricted waters) and for the open sea.

- Before leaving port, the master needs to satisfy himself that the vessel is equipped with the necessary charts and hydro-graphic publications for safe navigation.

- In particular, he should ensure that the vessel can be safely navigated at all times and in all areas of the intended passage.

- He is to verify that there shall always be adequate water under the vessel's keel, that there shall be no air draft restrictions in the ports or approaches to ports that he shall be entering, and that the intended courses do not take the vessel through restricted or hazardous areas.

- The initial courses to be followed are to be laid on the chart prior to leaving port.

- If the master delegates this duty to a navigating officer, he is to personally check them before sailing.

- If he lays the courses off himself, then one of the navigating officers should check with him before the ship leaves port.

- The information provided in Instructions for the passage plan should be used.

- Whenever compiling a voyage plan, the following plan may be used as a basis.

7.2. Passage Planning

- The master shall prepare a plan for the intended voyage before sailing.

- He may delegate preparing the plan to the second officer.

- The navigating officer shall extend or amend the original plan as appropriate if the port of destination changes.

7.3. Duties of the Officer on Watch

- Under no circumstances shall the officer on watch leave the bridge without being properly relieved.

- With the master present, he continues to be responsible for safety and navigation of the vessel until such time that the master informs him specifically that he shall assume the responsibility.

- The officer on watch shall not hand over the watch if he feels that the relieving officer is not capable of performing his watch duties (e.g. illness, under the influence of liquor or drugs, fatigued, etc.).

- The officer on watch shall defer the handing over of duty to the relieving officer if a maneuver or action to avoid a hazard is taking place, and until such action is complete.

- The officer on watch shall check and compare the vessel track and detailed plan. He shall then apply necessary alterations to the course to avoid possible errors that will cause disastrous consequences.

- The officer on watch shall refer to the master's bridge standing orders and night orders book.

7.4. Pilot Station to Berth

- The officer on duty, upon the pilot's arrival on board, shall present the pilot card to get the pilot familiarized with vessel particulars.

- In addition, the master shall advise the pilot of the vessel's maneuvering characteristics and basic details of the vessel's present condition along with his navigational intentions.

- The responsibility for navigation is not handed over to the pilot.

- The master and the watch officer retain all their duties and obligations.

- The officer on duty should co-operate closely with the pilot to assist him where possible and to maintain an accurate check on the ship's position, movements, and/or mark timings when passing channel buoys.

- The officer on watch shall inform the master immediately if he is in doubt of the pilot's actions or intentions.

- The officer on watch shall switch one radar to standby position to use as a reserve in case the radar in operation breaks down.

7.5. Calling the Master

- The officer on watch shall call the master anytime during heavy traffic, in an area navigating under restricted visibility, or in any other situation where he is in doubt.

- In addition, he shall refer to the master's bridge standing orders, night order book and ICS bridge procedure guide.

7.6. Vessel Squat

- Is the algebraic sum of the hull sinkage and the trimming effect generally occurring when the ship is moving forward into the shallow water?

- The officer on watch shall compute vessel squat and consider under keel clearance to the area navigated.

- Full form vessels such as tankers are associated with high block coefficients.

- Vessels with block coefficients higher than 0.7 will have the tendency to trim by the bow when squatting.

- The master shall reduce vessel speed when navigating into shallow water in order to increase under keel clearance.

7.7. Parallel Index Plotting

- A line drawn from echo tangential to the variable range marker circle set to the desired distance.

- The officer on watch during coastal navigation should set the radar parallel index to the desired safe distance. This is done in order to monitor how much the vessel is off track from the course laid up on the chart.

7.8. Course Alterations/Wheel Over Positions

- The officer on watch shall execute 20 degrees port and starboard wheel over position when altering course in order to control immediate vessel swinging.

- This is done also to avoid increase in main engine load that may cause turbocharger surging.

- The recommendation does not impede using hard over if deemed necessary

7.9. Course Alterations/Radar Range and Bearing

Lists of identified conspicuous points of landmarks or charted objects to use as reference for altering courses at every waypoint.

7.10. Cross Track Margin

- The Master should note safe cross track margins for the desired route plan at every point.

- It is the vessel port and starboard cross track error from the ideal track with effects from currents, wind, and traffic avoidance.

- The officer on duty shall in every possible way maintain the vessel on the course line laid out by the chart by correcting cross track errors once vessel position is acquired and plotted.

7.11. Weather

- The officer on duty shall, upon receipt of the weather fax or CW from the radio officer, read and sign for acknowledgement.

- For reference, consult sailing directions and pilot charts.

7.12. Tidal Streams/Currents

- The Officer on Watch shall check current rate and directions of the area navigated.

- For reference, consult sailing directions and pilot chart.

Chapter 8: Ship Crew Duties During the Repair & Dry Dock

This chapter has been produced in order to introduce to SRM the ship crew responsibilities on-board ship from entering the dry dock to sail-out from the yard.

8.1. General

- Prior to carrying out major repairs and/or dry docking the ship, there are a number of considerations to bear in mind as outlined in the following paragraphs.

- The Company is responsible for ensuring that each vessel is dry-docked in accordance with Classification Society's rules.

- Special circumstances may occur that require the scheduled docking to be brought forward or deferred.

- In this case, the company advises the vessel's owner and makes the necessary arrangements.

- Major refits may be required as a result of unforeseen damage, changes to International rules and regulations, or major modifications required by the vessel's owner.

- The advice of defect system of reporting is maintained. Each vessel's master/chief engineer reports, as necessary, any defects or repairs for inclusion in the docking specification.

- The S/E prepares a full docking specification against information obtained from:

  o Classification Society requirements
  o Owners requirements
  o Inspection reports
  o Planned maintenance reports
  o Advice of defects report
  o Incident/damage reports
  o Masters/Chief Engineers reports
  o Changes in legislation, national, port state, and International.

- The docking/refit specification contains advice on the vessel's date of availability and defines the work to be covered in the following areas:

  o General services
  o Dry-docking
  o Hull preparation
  o Painting
  o Steel repairs/renewals
  o Deck repairs

- o Engine repairs
- o Electrical repairs
- o Accommodation repairs
- o Outside contractors
- o Surveys

- The completed specification is checked for accuracy and detail and then presented to the technical manager for authorization.

- If required, a copy is forwarded to the vessel's owner.

- Once the quotation is approved by the technical manager, the authorized specification is tendered to several company approved shipyards for quotation.

- A comparison summary containing all anticipated expenditure, authorized by the technical manager, with the company recommended yard is forwarded to the vessel's owner for authorizations.

- On receipt of the owner's written approval, the technical manager or his designated SE to the selected yard awards the contract.

8.2. Inspection and Verification

- All dry-docking/major refits are attended by at least one company superintendent and/or a representative nominated by the technical manager.

- In conjunction with the company representative, the vessel's senior officers monitor the work carried out on board for compliance with the repair specification.

- The progress of the docking/repair is monitored at a daily meeting attended by both company representatives and responsible shipyard personnel. This meeting ensures that resources are allocated in the most effective manner to enable completion of the docking/repair within time and budgetary limits.

- All maintenance work carried out by ships staff or sub-contractors is recorded in the VFS on board and by the company.

8.3. Reporting

- The attending S/E forwards progress/status reports, in writing, to the company and owners as required by the technical manager.

- On completion of the docking, a full dry-dock repair report is prepared.

- This report is forwarded to the owner and copies kept in the VFS on board and by the company.

- A dry docking/repair analysis form is prepared and forwarded to the owner if required and kept in the VFS on board and by the company.

8.4. Alterations of Fittings

- No structural alterations to the vessel or her fittings, including the re-locating of safety equipment, shall be made without the sanction of the company.

- Should this sanction be obtained then the master and the chief engineer must ensure that the appropriate drawings on board are correctly amended.

- Copies of amended drawings must be forwarded to the company with all changes highlighted in order for the office copies of the same drawings to be similarly amended.

- Stability information must reflect any substantial changes BEFORE the vessel leaves the shipyard or repair berth.

- The master and the C/E must liase with the company on this matter as a matter of extreme importance.

- Additional steelwork may result in the requirement for an inclining experiment to be carried out.

8.5. Supervision of Repairs

- It is usual for all work in connection with the dry-docking, repair, and upkeep of the ship to be carried out under the supervision of the vessel's S/E.

- Additions to the original specification shall not be put in hand without the permission of the TM or the company.

- It is the responsibility of the vessel's staff to thoroughly test and prove satisfactory all repairs and for quality control and report any defects to the TM.

- Regular meetings between the vessel's senior officers, superintendent, and repairer are held to monitor work progress, discuss difficulties, and work schedule.

8.6. Dry Docking

- Before entry into dry-dock, the C/E is responsible for ensuring that the bilge wells and engine room tank tops are dry and that all double bottom tank lids are in place and secured.

- Fire pumps, sanitary pumps, and sewage unit pumps are to be isolated when the vessel is dry-docked and the shore fire main has been connected.

- Before the vessel enters dry dock, the C/E and C/O must discuss and decide upon the distribution of both ballast and bunkers to obtain the correct docking condition and thus avoid undue stress to the hull when the vessel takes the blocks. Records of the draft forward and aft, and the ullages or dips of water or oil in double bottom tanks, peaks, cofferdams and bunker compartments, must be entered in the E/R and deck log books.

8.7. Dry Dock Inspection

When the dock is dry, the outside and bottom of the hull, propeller, rudder etc. must be inspected by the master, chief Engineer and the company's representative to ascertain the condition and if any damage has been sustained since the previous docking.

8.8. Gas Free Certificate

- During repair periods no space is to be considered gas free unless a gas free certificate has been obtained and maintained.

- The certificate must state whether the space is gas free for hot work or entry only.

8.9. Boiler Blow Down

When it is necessary to steam a boiler during dry dockings, the blow down valves and cocks must be secured to prevent accidental discharge into the dry dock.

8.10. Undocking

- Prior to flooding the dock, the C/E and master will satisfy themselves that all drain plugs are properly fitted and that all sea valves are shut.

- All such plugs should be held by C/O while being removed.

- Distribution of weight and trim of the ship must be the same on leaving dry dock as on entering.

- Special sanction must be obtained from the S/E in charge of repairs and from the docking authorities for any departure from this instruction.

- The C/E is to station officers to inspect all sea connections and hull repairs while the dry dock is being flooded.

- Flooding is to be stopped before the vessel lifts off the blocks and a full examination is to be carried out to ensure that the vessel is watertight.

Author References

OCEAN US CO..LTD.
#1480-7, Jung-dong, Haeundae-gu, Busan, Korea
Tel +82 51 790 1700 | Fax +82 51 790 1795
www.ocean-us.co.kr | E-mail: sales@ocean-us.co.kr

Attn. Marketing Department
Oman Drydock Company (ODC)

29th of Nov, 2012

LETTER FOR APPRECIATION

In grateful appreciation of Invaluable support and unstinted cooperation extended for the successful implementation of the HL5000 Project, herein we officially deliver our appreciation to **Mr. Mohamed Khamis (ODC Ship Repair Manager)** for his dedication to the HL5000 during whole period of the project.

His confidence and long-term experience on ship repair work has brought flawless quality and time reducing delivery by leading each department to the same commitment resulting in incredible success of the project.

All jobs were carefully controlled by **Mr. Mohamed Khamis** with sufficient knowledge of this unique HL5000 system, and entire yard enthusiastically backed up outstanding issues.

We are confident that both **Mr. Mohamed Khamis** and **Oman Drydock Company (ODC)** have stepped up to the next level, not only technical aspect also management of such a vast project through HL5000 project.

It will be our pleasure to work again with ODC, under his management in the near future.

Further, I would be delighted if you kindly forward a copy of this letter to him.

Thank you & Best regards

Dae-Gyun Woo

HL5000 Project Manager
OCEANUS CO., LTD.

OCEANUS CO.,LTD.

121

Marine Logistic Solutions LLC
P.O. Box 31966, Dubai, U.A.E.
Tel.   : +971 4 2971912
Fax   : +971 4 2970147
E-mail : marsol@etasnp.com
Website : www.marsol.ae

الـجــلــول الــبـحـريــة (ذ.م.م)
ص.ب : ٣١٩٦٦ دبي، إ.ع.م.م
الهاتف : +٩٧١ ٤ ٢٩٧١٩١٢
الفاكس : +٩٧١ ٤ ٢٩٧٠١٤٧
البريد الالكتروني : marsol@etasnp.com
موقع الإنترنت : www.marsol.ae

Date:22nd June, 2008

LETTER OF APPRECIATION

MarSol XI (AHTS) has undergone for the major repairs due fire in the Engine room at Arab Shipbuilding & Repair Yard (ASRY), Bahrain from 29 Oct 2007 to June 2008

There were several jobs which were undertaken particularly in Engine room, wheel house & accommodation.

All the jobs were very professionally completed by the staff of the yard in the absence of many drawings & manuals maintaining all the quality and standards.

Therefore I would like to acknowledge and appreciate the efforts **Supervised by Mr. Mohamed Khamis Mohamed / Ship Repair Manager** in preparing our vessel once again ready to operate safely.

Further, I extend my warm greetings to **Mr. Mohamed Khamis Mohamed** on behalf of Marine Logistics Solutions L.L.C, Dubai.

The commercial department is requested to handover this letter to the concerned person

Thanks & Regards,

Fuad Hashmi
General Manager – Technical & Operations
ETA MarSol
P.O.Box 31966
Dubai

Oil & Gas   Dredging & Reclamation   Marine Construction   Tug & Barge

E T A   S T A R   G R O U P

 Dutch Dredging BV.

TSHD SEINE.

ALEXANDRIA DD EGYPT

From Mike E Roberts

Superintendent for TSHD Seine

TO: Eng. Rabie Abd El Raouf Mohamed (Director of Ship repair)

ALEXANDRIA SHIPYARD EGYPT

03rd December 2009

Ref: Ship Repair Manager Mr. Mohamed Khamis Mohamed.

Dear Sir,

I wish to thank Mr. Mohamed Khamis Mohamed for his outstanding assistance and technical knowledge over the past two months. With his excellent command of English and his own language he has been a great help to me over this period and I have enjoyed working with him.
I hope I will have the pleasure to work with him as my ship repair manager on my next visit to your shipyard.

NB: I would be grateful if you would kindly forward a copy of this letter to him.

Mike Roberts

Superintendent

M/T CHRYSSI

Date: 17.03.2013

From: Capt. Markos (Owner Represintative).

To: Mr. C.G. Choi (ODC Production Director).

CC: Mr. S.H. Choi (ODC Marketing Director).

Letter of Appreciation

M/T CHRYSSI Is Belong To AVIN International S.A. Co. & She Was Undergoing For Special Survey at

Oman Dry Dock Co. Under Commend Of Mr. Mohamed Khamis (Yard Ship Repair Manager).

All the Works Were Carrying out Perfectly & Safely under His Good Supervision, So For This Reason I

would Like To Extend My Warm Greeting To Him & On Behalf of "AVIN" Company I would Like To

Recommend Him As our Ship Repair Manager On-board Our Ships On Next Visit To Oman Dry Dock

Co.

Many Thanks & Best Regard,,,,,,,,,,,

Capt.: Markos Karvounis

AVIN Owner Represintative

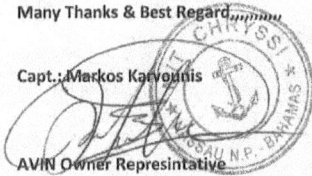

Appreciation Letter for Collaboration

We have been working with Mr. Mohammed Ahmed Khamis on and off since 2016 with the purpose of establishing a long-term relationship and contract between ODC and ABB. During this time, we have found him to be consistently loyal, dedicated to ODC and in particular skillful with Contracts Management.

Our Department is responsible for the after sales service of ABB Turbochargers in the UAE, various Gulf countries, Egypt, Pakistan and Afghanistan. From our offices in the UAE we coordinate and carry out the sales of spare parts, services in our workshops and at sites on board of vessels as well as power plants and railway applications.

We have found Mr. Mohammed Khamis to be very interested and helpful in formulating the contract enabling ABB to set up a Turbocharging Service Point within Oman Drydocks Company. His engagement to find a pleasing solution for all involved parties was much appreciated.

We would recommend Mr. Mohammed Khamis to any potential employer at any time. We thank him for his commitment, and wish him all the best for his future.

Sincerely,

EDI FIOR
Name
Local Business Unit Manager
Title/Duty
Thursday, June 08, 2017
Date and Signature

SHIBU RAJAMANI
Name
Regional Business Development Manager
Title/Duty
Thursday, June 08, 2017
Date and Signature

ABB Industries (L.L.C)
Turbocharging
Behind Tasjeel Traffic Department
4th Interchange, Al Quoz
P.O. Box 11070
Dubai, United Arab Emirates

Phone +971 4 314 7500
Fax: +971 4 340 1771
E-Mail: turbo@ae.abb.com
www.abb.com/turbocharging

1/1

Consilium

Letter of Appreciation

We are Consilium Middle East, Dubai would like to extend our appreciation to **Mr. Mohamed Khamis/ Technical sources Strategy Planner** with ODC for his plan assistance for getting long term contract with Oman Dry Dock Company (ODC), Duqm at Sultanate of Oman.

His perfect technical knowledge, negotiation skill for the commercial issue was helpful for finalizing the draft agreement with Oman Dry Dock Company.

It is our pleasure to give him this appreciation letter & wish him all the best.

Best Regards,

Name: **Madan Kumar**

Position: **Area Manager**

Signature:

Consilium Stamp.

Consilium Engineering & Trading LLC
C.R 1157672, P.O.Box.159, PC -101
Sultanate of Oman

كونسيليوم للهندسة والتجارة ش ذ م م
سي ار: 1157672, س ب: 159, بي سي 101
سلطنة عمان

126

شركة عُمان للأحواض الجافة ش.م.ع.ع.
OMAN DRYDOCK COMPANY, S.A.O.C.

Certificates of appreciation

Present to

ENG. MOHAMED KHAMIS MOHAMED AHMED

From SRM Department to the outstanding efforts made during the last period of the success of the projects entrusted to it, and look forward to further excellence and achievement.

Emil Chivu
Head of SRM

S.J Park
Production Director

Date: 23rd June 2014

127

ASRY

ARAB SHIPBUILDING AND REPAIR YARD CO

الشركة العربية لبناء واصلاح السفن

التاريخ: 4 أغسطس 2008

شهادة خدمة
Service Certificate

Name :	:	Mohamed Khamis Mohamed Ahmed	: الاسم
	:	24100	: رقم شارة العمل
Nationality	:	Egyptian	: الجنسية
Position :	:	Shiprepair Manager	: الوظيفة
CPR No	:	760240787	: رقم السجل السكاني
GOSI No.			: رقم التأمين الاجتماعي
Period of Service			مدة الخدمة
From	:	5ᵗʰ August, 2006	: من
To	:	4ᵗʰ August, 2008	: إلى

To obtain further information if any, please write directly to our Personnel Administration Service.

للحصول على مزيد من المعلومات يرجى الكتابة مباشرة إلى خدمات شئون الموظفين.

عن الشركة العربية لبناء وإصلاح السفن
For Arab Shipbuilding & Repair Yard Co.

شركة شئون الموظفين
Personnel Administration Supervisor

P.O. Box : 50110, Hidd
Kingdom of Bahrain
Tel. : (+973) 671111
Fax : (+973) 670236
E-mail : asryco@batelco.com.bh
Web Site : www.asry.net

ص.ب : 50110 - الحد
مملكة البحرين
هاتف: 671111 (973+)
فاكس: 670236 (973+)
البريد الإلكتروني: asryco@batelco.com.bh
Web Site : www.asry.net

DNV

ISO 9001 & 14001 REGISTERED FIRM

128

MAHONEY

SHIPPING & MARINE SERVICES

TO WHOM IT MAY CONCERN

We, Mahoney shipping and marine services certifies that :

Eng. : **Mohamed Khamis Mohamed Ahmed**   *Spent 7 Months*

(from *01/03/2009* To *30/09/2009*)

As assistance superintendent engineer

His performance was excellent and highly appreciated.

" This certificate was issued upon his request with no responssibility

or obligation from us."

MAHONEY
SHIPPING & MARINE SERVICES

HUMAN RESOURCES & ADMINISTRATION
AFFAIRS MANAGER
NAME:
SIGN.:
DATE   30/09/2009

NOTE:
Any abrasion or change in the data in this document will hold it to be void even if it is accredited

ORIGINAL : EMPLOYEE   COPY : HR DEPT. (EMPLOYEE'S FILE)

ماهوني للخدمات الملاحية والبحرية

31 Soltan Hossein St, 21519 Alexandria ; Egypt. P.O. Box: 629. Tel. +203 4831000 (8 Lines) - Fax +203 4832000 www.mahoneyegypt.com
Cairu - Damietta - Port said

Khaled kotb
Chief Estimator at Heavy
Engineering Industries
Shipbuilding Co. (HEISCO)

May 14, 2017, Eng. Mohamed
worked with Khaled in the same
group

Worked with Mr. Mohamed Khamism for years in Arab
Shipbuilding & Repair Yard (ASRY).
He was the dedicated & committed one for the job.
Always keen about targets & jobs completion.
And Commercially always keeping an eye on cost to minimize it.
Was nice working together as a Team.

Alexandru Dumitru
Technical Operations
Manager

September 21, 2011, Alexandru
managed Eng. Mohamed directly

Mohamed have good pro-active mind.trying all the time to find
right solution for daily issues.With good technical background he
provide trust in our team.

Asry Alaa Bishawi
SHIP MANAGER at ASRY

September 20, 2011, Asry Alaa
was senior to Eng. Mohamed but

Was a hard working. Building his ability. Improving his planning.

www.ingramcontent.com/pod-product-compliance
Lightning Source LLC
Chambersburg PA
CBHW061752270326
41928CB00011B/2469